QUAYSIDE & WAREHOUSE FIXTURES

IN LIVERPOOL'S SOUTH DOCKS

Drawings: Nick Phillips

Text: David Cropper, Paul Derby, Nancy Ritchie-Noakes

Editor: David Samuels

Merseyside County Museums

@ Copyright 1983

ISBN 0 906367 19 0

Set in Whittaker Cheltenham by
CPS Ltd., Liverpool

Printed by
Printfine Ltd., Liverpool

Designed by Barrie Jones

Contents

Preface

The Merseyside-Docklands History Survey was established in 1981 to undertake an industrial archaeological and historical survey of the South Docks in Liverpool. The project was sponsored by Merseyside County Museums and funded by the Manpower Services Commission and Merseyside Development Corporation.

The opening of Merseyside Maritime Museum at Canning Dock in the South Docks in 1980 heralded a new life for Livepool's historic docklands. The Maritime Museum, part of Merseyside County Museums, recognised early that site recording and interpretation were necessary as both a service to museum visitors and a scholarly responsibility. The Merseyside Docklands History Survey has used written, drawn, photographic and oral archives to illuminate the history of the South Docks; the industrial archaeology of these docks has been investigated by means of building and artefact surveys which have been recorded on drawings and in photographs.

The nature of docks is such that they supply a great number of subjects and objects which require study in depth; these may be studied chronologically, functionally, spatially or structurally. To publish the results of one of the Docklands History Survey's studies — a survey of quayside and warehouse fixtures — is to illustrate the variety of extant industrial archaeological material and to provide a compact record of interest to all who are concerned with the recording, interpretation, protection or re-use of historic industrial places.

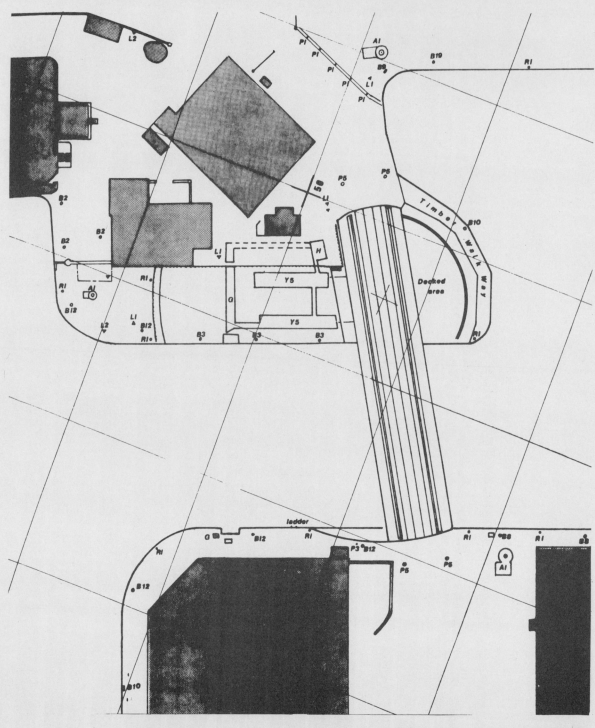

4

Figure 1 Wapping Queens Passage. Extract from the 1:500 map, produced by the MDHB, to show the positions of all structures and artefacts visible at quay level on the South Docks.

1.0 Introduction

As its title suggests, the Merseyside Docklands History Survey was set up to investigate the history of the docks in the port of Liverpool along the River Mersey. The first geographical area to be studied was that known as the South Docks in Liverpool, which extends from the present day Pier Head in the north to Herculaneum Dock in the south. The survey area comprised some 130 acres of disused docks which had been closed to commercial shipping in 1972 and which were vested in Merseyside Development Corporation in 1981. The research programme was designed to yield descriptions of the planning, design, construction, operation and re-construction of the dock system which dates from 1708. Sources available for consultation included the County Museum's enormously valuable Mersey Docks and Harbour Board Collection of manuscripts, drawings, printed material and photographs; the City Libraries' municipal records and local history collection; other documentary sources lodged in company archives, private libraries and record offices; oral histories; and the structures and artefacts which remain in dockland.

The use of sources and techniques was tailored to individual topics and sites. Although nearly three centuries of rebuilding, repair and maintenance have destroyed or obscured much of the physical evidence of the history of the docks, much of value remains. The Mersey Docks and Harbour Board (now Mersey Docks and Harbour Co) owned and developed almost all of the Liverpool and Birkenhead Docks from 1858 until 1981. The Board's predecessor from 1708 was a trust formed from the members of the Town Council. This long-term corporate ownership and management prevented the fragmentation of the docks and dispersal of their records. The security maintained on the dock estate while it was in use protected the built environment from vandalism, thereby ensuring an inheritance of physical remains.

1.1 Historical Background

Liverpool's first wet dock was built between 1709 and 1721 at the mouth of a tidal inlet known as the Pool. The dock was made by reclaiming part of the foreshore of the River Mersey and impounding water within man-made walls and behind a pair of mitre gates. It was not a very sophisticated development, in engineering terms, but it constituted a dramatic improvement in ship and cargo handling in the port of Liverpool. The Mersey has a tidal range of over 30 ft, and navigation of the river — affected by strong currents, shifting sand banks and powerful winds — has never been easy. The construction of a wet dock which afforded a safe haven for shipping was a significant advance: berthed in a dock, ships could be loaded and discharged without regard to the state of the tide. Small craft no longer had to take the ground at the ebb of the tide, and larger vessels no longer needed to anchor in the river to be loaded and unloaded by means of tenders.

Ship-handling and cargo-handling aids antedate dock construction by many centuries, but the development of a variety of increasingly sophisticated mechanical aids was roughly contemporaneous with the development of wet dock systems. The ever larger scale of operations demanded a corresponding increase in the power to do work in the docks. The mechanical advantage which could be gained by the use of gears in machines was the first to be exploited. The development of steam driven cranes speeded cargo-handling, but the leap from manual to powered operation of dock gates and machines did not come until the introduction of hydraulic power. Gas was used mainly to fuel lights and heaters, although from the 1890's it did power some belt driven machinery at the Coburg Dockyard. When electric power was introduced it was utilised to operate cranes and capstans. Today the modern port of Liverpool is worked electrically and hydraulically, and, although fluid other than water has sometimes been used in hydraulic gate machinery, the principles of operation remain unchanged and unchallenged by any other kind of power.

Hydraulic power was introduced to the Liverpool docks in 1874 when W G Armstrong, the Newcastle lawyer-turned-inventor, supplied an hydraulic hoist for installation in the South Stack of the new Albert Dock Warehouses. This was the world's first hydraulic lift. By 1850 Armstrong had perfected the design for a power storage facility, known as an accumulator, which obviated the need to depend on mains water supplies and which provided water under much higher pressures than those obtainable from a gravity-feed system. The first working accumulator was installed in 1851 at the premises of the Manchester, Sheffield and Lincoln Railway at New Holland, Humberside, and a little later accumulators were provided on the Liverpool dock estate. One of the first sites for the new machinery in Liverpool was the Stanley Dock, where two accumulators were installed to supply pressure water to a variety of cargo handling appliances. Hydraulic power was not applied to the dock gates there, even though the construction of the dock was concurrent with that of the hydraulic installation. Hydraulic power centres, each typically consisting of a prime mover (usually a steam engine), pump, acculator and reservoir were built subsequently at Wapping (1856), Toxteth (1890) and Herculaneum (1900) Docks. Albert Dock's extant hydraulic power centre was erected in 1878, replacing an earlier 'engine house' whose site and precise function have not yet been ascertained. Near the end of the nineteenth century, the Albert and Wapping power stations were closed, and the hydraulic machinery in these docks was thenceforth run from the other centres to the south.

Despite ever more technological advances in the design of docks and machinery, manpower dominated dock operation. Not only were men needed to work the available machines, but they were also used to do jobs then beyond the capacity of mechanical handling. Sometimes men were used because they were just as efficient as machines — and cheaper. As late as the 1930's, bulk shipments of loose Brazil nuts were man-handled from ships into the Kings Dock transit sheds where they were shovelled into sacks before being weighed and distributed.

Dockland jobs became more specialised as the volume of business and its attendant complexities increased.

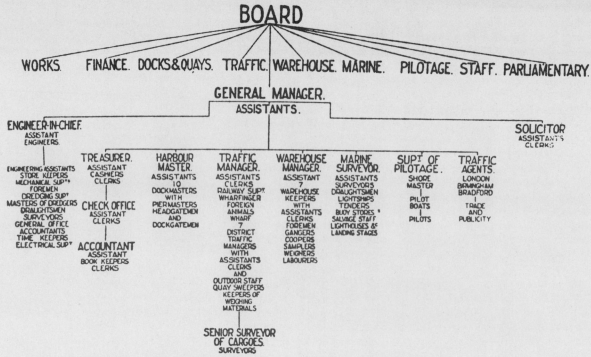

Figure 2 MDHB Management Structure, 1947.

From the day in 1724 when Thomas Steers, Liverpool's first dock engineer, was appointed Dock Master and Water Bailiff by the Corporation of Liverpool, the staff of the dock estate's managing body burgeoned. In 1761 the Corporation, recognising that port management was distinct from their other functions, established the Dock Committee, and eventually a governing body entirely separaté from the Corporation, the Mersey Docks and Harbour Board, was constituted to conduct the affairs of the port. The Board, of twenty eight members was served by several committees, each of which dealt with one aspect of the dock estate's management. Although the Board employed a large labour force including professional men, tradespeople and administrators (see fig 2), the majority of stevedores, porters and dock labourers were employed on a casual basis by shipowners, their agents and other private companies. H M Customs and Immigration Officers and the representatives of shipping lines and railway companies also worked along the waterfront. At the end of World War II, 1 in 3 of Merseyside workers were employed on the docks. Now that the port of Liverpool's share of maritime trade has diminished, and modern technology has made work much less labour intensive, the ships and the men have deserted the South Docks. Only the fabric and fixtures of the place remain.

1.2 Method of Survey and Record

A primary objective of the Merseyside Docklands History Survey was to record the South Docks site, closed to commercial shipping in 1972 and opened to redevelopment in 1982. Site surveys took several forms. Basic coverage of superficial features throughout the survey area was recorded on Council for British Archaeology Industrial Archaeology Report Cards which when completed provide a brief written description of the

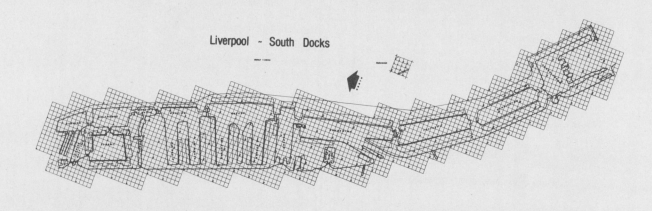

Figure 3 Liverpool South Docks. 1:0000 reduced reproduction of the 1:5000 base map used in the site survey.

site, building, artefact or fixture, its location (National Grid Reference and unique sequential number) and 35mm black and white photograph of it. Measured surveys or dimensioned sketches were made of selected buildings or parts of buildings; choice of subject for this treatment was governed by rarity, linkage to preceding or succeeding structures or the threat of demolition. Merseyside Development Corporation made available to the Docklands Survey copies of structural and architectural surveys commissioned by the Corporation. A comprehensive 35mm photographic survey, comprising some 4,000 photographs of exterior features, was also compiled; the photographic record includes coverage of selected interiors and some machinery details. Coverage of subjects which required professional photography — such as the eighteenth century Dukes Dock wall and interiors of the Albert Dock Warehouses — was arranged by the Royal Commission on Historical Monuments (England).

All of the site survey material is keyed to a 1:5,000 base map sub-divided to 25m squares (see fig 3), each of which has a unique number. Each 100m square, based on the Ordnance Survey 1:1,250 grid, has a sequential number, and every 25m square within it is identified by the 100m square number and an affix from 1 to 16 (see fig 4). Eight 1:500 sheets cover the South Docks (see fig 1 which is a full size extract from the 1:500 sheet showing the Wapping — Queens passage. On these sheets are plotted the positions of all structures and artefacts visible from quay level. All of the fixtures are labelled, by means of a letter-number code, as to type. The types are illustrated by photographs and by drawings to scale; as it was not usually possible to excavate the fixtures, they have been illustrated as they appear from the quay surface. The photographic archive is arranged by dock name and its contents are listed to give National Grid Reference, M D H S 1:5,000 reference number, negative number and a brief written description of subject.

In general, culverts, sluices, chain holes and the like were not recorded or investigated because of restrictions imposed by safety considerations. Many buildings in the South Docks were still in use at the time of survey, and access difficulties precluded most interior work. Time, too, was limited.

The letter-number identification code (such as B12 or W3), used to differentiate fixture types, is based on sequence of find, from south to north in the South Docks. It does not indicate chronological or technological sequence. In this publication, the decimal prefix to the letter-number codes is intended to relate, where applicable, to technological development; the progression from low numbers to higher numbers generally reflects the progression from simple to more sophisticated technology. Thus fixture 3.1 is likely to be a forerunner of fixture 3.9. The classification, nevertheless, is not straightforward. In some cases, there has been no measurable technological advance, but simply a change in design. Moreover, because of technological anachronisms, fixtures in the catalogue have not been arranged according to date of installation. Information about dating, function and use of the dockland fixtures has been culled from the Docklands Survey Union Catalogue and from published secondary sources. Examples outside the survey area were considered but not recorded.

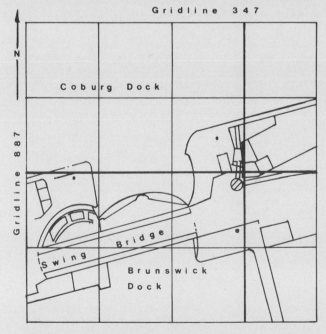

Figure 4 Coburg-Brunswick Passage. Extract from the 1:1250 map showing 100 metre grid (thick lines) and 25 metre grid (thin lines).

2.0 Mooring posts and bollards

The first mooring posts were made of hardwood and later, ships made fast to stone posts and even to old cannon which had been buried muzzle downwards. But since the beginning of the nineteenth century, quay edges have been fitted with cast iron and then cast steel bollards designed for increasingly specialised ship-handling and ship-holding. The shapes of bollards indicate their function.

A circular section bollard [2.1(B.1)] is generally installed at dock entrances where the friction afforded by several turns of rope around the bollard is used to check a vessel's way as it is warped through a dock passage. Because of the powerful forces exerted on a bollard in this position, this type is often set as much as 5 ft below the surface of the quay. Type 2.1(B.1) is hollow; the walls are 1 in thick.

Mooring bollards are characterised by their asymmetric lips provided to hold fast the ropes from ships whose decks are high above the quay. Types 2.8(B8), 2.12(B12) and 2.14(B14) are 'Liverpool pattern' mooring posts which are sometimes filled with concrete through the core hole at the top. The lips on these bollards would be an impediment and a danger on a warping bollard which has to facilitate the rapid coiling and uncoiling of ropes. Bollards at graving docks may combine the features of warping types and mooring types; in these cases the slow operating speed compensates for the presence of lips on the bollards.

Where many barges or other relatively small craft frequent a dock, small bollards called dollies are fixed in the quay [2.23(B23), 2.24(B24) and 2.26(B26)]. The T-shape bollards [2.9(B9)] and 2.10(B10)] have a hollow top section through which a chain can be run if necessary. Quay level flanges are cast on some bollards, giving extra strength at the point of maximum stress and reducing rope abrasion. Various accessories including fencing chain holders, rope holders and pegs (illustrated) are commonly fitted to many of the nineteenth century bollards.

Table 1 shows a compilation of forces, acting in respect of different vessel weights, giving figures for the force on the bollard, the bollard force on the quay, and the bollard force parallel to the quay.

Table 1

Total Weight of Vessel (Tons)	Bollard Force (Tons)	Bollard Force on Quay (Tons per foot)	Bollard Force Parallel to the Quay (Tons per foot)
2,000	10	0.46	0.31
5,000	20	0.46	0.31
10,000	30	0.62	0.46
20,000	50	0.77	0.62

Bollard Data

Table 2

Identification code	B	Material Used	Height above quay	Diameter at base	Approx date of installation of South Docks (where available)
2.1	1	Cast Iron	3ft	9in	1851
2.2	2	Cast Iron	2ft 8in	9in	1834
2.3	3	Cast Iron	7½in	5in	
2.4	4	Cast Iron	1ft 4in	5in	
2.5	5	Cast Iron	2ft 2in	12in	
2.6	6	Cast Iron	1ft	7in	
2.7	7	Cast Iron	1ft 5in	8in	
2.8	8	Cast Iron	2ft	11in	c1900
2.9	9	Cast Iron	1ft 4in	7in	
2.10	10	Cast Iron	1ft	6in	
2.11	11	Cast Iron	1ft 4in	12in square	
2.12	12	Cast Iron	2ft	13in	
2,13	13	Cast Iron	2ft	10in	
2.14	14	Cast Iron	2ft	12in	
2.15	15	Cast Iron	1ft 10in	10in	
2.16	16	Cast Iron	2ft 4in	9in	
2.17	17	Steel	1ft 8in	15in square	c1920
2.18	18	Cast Iron	2ft 10in	12in	
2.19	19	Cast Iron	1ft 2in	8in	
2.20	20	Cast Iron	2ft 2in	9in	
2.21	21	Cast Iron	1ft	8in	
2.22	22	Steel	8in	6in	
2.23	23	Steel	1ft	4in	
2.24	24	Cast Iron	1ft 2in	5in	
2.25	25	Cast Iron	1ft 2in	8in	
2.26	26	Steel	6in	4in	
2.27	27	Steel	9in	7in	
2.28	28	Cast Iron	10in	7in	
2.29	29	Cast Iron	1ft 7in	7in	
2.30	30	Cast Iron	2ft	9in	1834

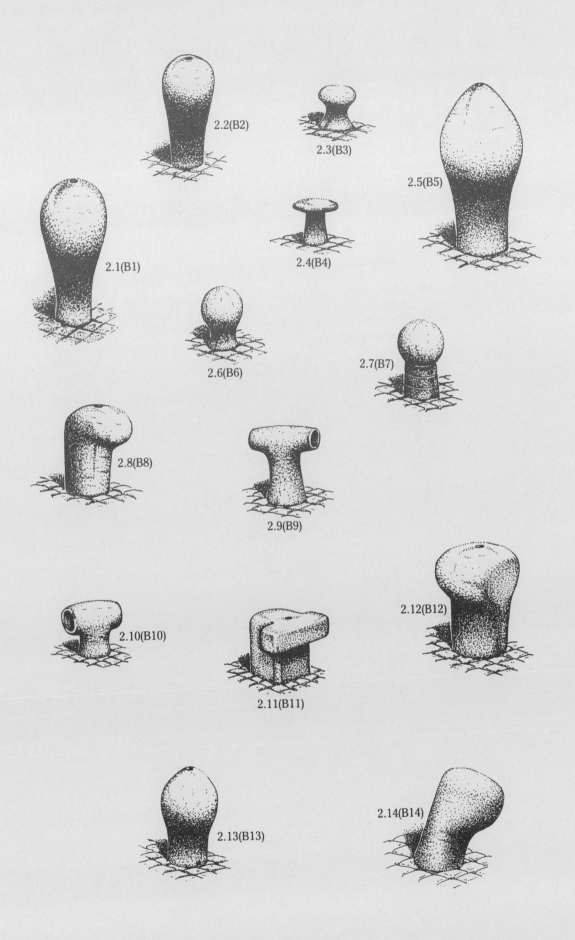

2.2(B2)

2.3(B3)

2.5(B5)

2.1(B1)

2.4(B4)

2.6(B6)

2.7(B7)

2.8(B8)

2.9(B9)

2.10(B10)

2.11(B11)

2.12(B12)

2.13(B13)

2.14(B14)

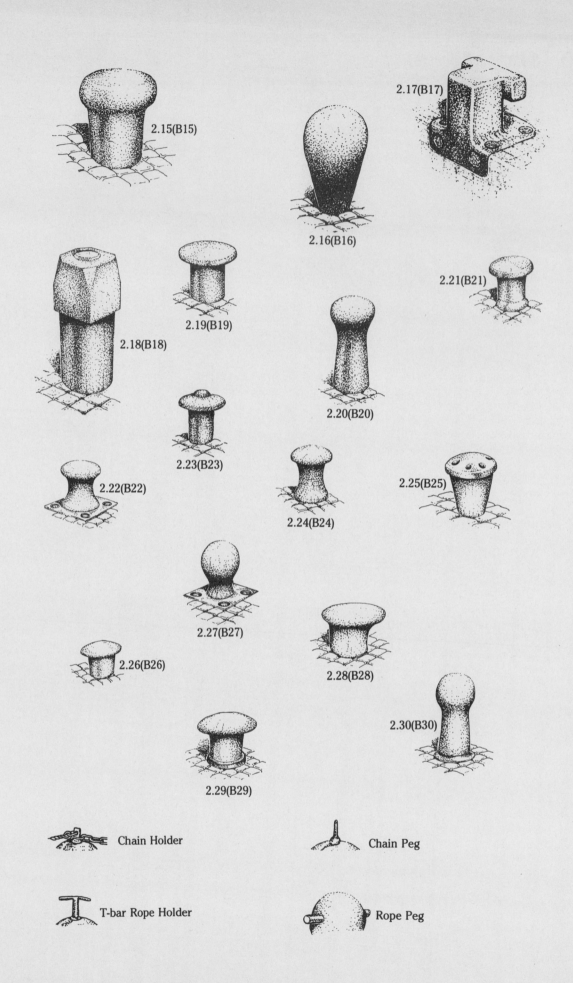

2.15(B15)

2.16(B16)

2.17(B17)

2.18(B18)

2.19(B19)

2.20(B20)

2.21(B21)

2.22(B22)

2.23(B23)

2.24(B24)

2.25(B25)

2.26(B26)

2.27(B27)

2.28(B28)

2.29(B29)

2.30(B30)

Chain Holder

Chain Peg

T-bar Rope Holder

Rope Peg

10

3.0 Capstans

Capstans were originally developed in conjunction with the increase in size and weight of anchors and yards which could not be handled using only blocks and tackle. Their use was logically extended from ships to quays; in the docks, capstans are used to manoeuvre ships and to haul railway trucks along wharves.

A capstan consists of a revolving vertical barrel surmounted by a circular drumhead. Early, manually operated capstans featured vertical whelps on the outer surface of the barrel and square holes in the perimeter of the drumhead. The whelps were provided to retard rope slippage, and the holes were provided to receive the ends of the ash or hickory capstan bars by which the capstan was turned. The whelps and bar holes were retained in some of the later, hydraulically powered machines, but the capstan form ultimately evolved had lost both of these features. The provision of bar sockets on hydraulic capstans enabled them to be used as hand capstans in the event of hydraulic power failure.

Most of the capstans remaining in the South Docks are made of cast iron, though there are one or two examples with wooden whelps and some made of steel. Those with wooden barrels which revolve on an iron spindle [3.1(A4)] are the oldest and the least sophisticated of the single purchase manual capstans. This type was worked by dockers pushing on the capstan bars as they walked round the capstan, on the same principle as a horse-mill. The pattern of the wooden whelp capstan was copied later on in iron, resulting in a machine which was as decorative as it was functional [see 3.2(A9)]. More sophisticated manual capstans [3.4(A3) and 3.5(A7)] had gears inside their drumheads at ratios of 4:1 and 3:1 respectively, (the older 3:1 design, with gears in the base of the barrel, is illustrated diagrammatically in fig 5). Most of the capstans illustrated have ratchet brakes fitted, some visibly, in order to prevent 'whiplash'.

W G Armstrong devised an hydraulically powered capstan which was worked by two or three in-line oscillating pistons driving cranks covering 180° or 120° of the circle respectively. Fig 6 shows an engine with three pistons, each operated by a valve. The reciprocating action is converted to rotary motion via a 'three throw crankshaft', which ensures easy starting, as only one of the pistons is fully extended at a time. Each valve is operated by a cam attached to its corresponding cylinder at the pivot point, the rocking motion of the cylinder causing the cam to activate the inlet and exhaust alternately. Some engines have two valves per cylinder (one for forward motion, one for reverse), and others have a single valve and reversing gears. Armstrong's development of direct-acting radial pistons, situated beneath the winding drum of the capstan, dispensed altogether with the need for gears. This latter arrangement was more efficient and less wasteful of space. A further refinement was obtained with the introduction of the turn-over type of capstan [3.9(A8)]which could be easily inverted for access to its hydraulic engine.

A typical three ton load hydraulic capstan could operate at a speed of 15rpm. Standard operating pressure was 750 pounds per sq in and when operating at full speed the capstan required some 35 gallons of water per minute.

In addition to capstan supplied by Sir William Armstrong, Whitworth & Co, Newcastle, those manufactured by C & A Musker, Bootle, [3.6(A1) and 3.7(A2)], Ogden & Barnes Ltd, Liverpool [3.4(A3) and 3.5(A7)], Tannett Walker & Co Ltd, Leeds [3.8(A5), Stothert & Pitt, Bath [3.10(A19)], John Abbot & Co Ltd, Gateshead [3.6(A1)], and Glenfield & Kennedy, Kilmarnock [3.9(A8)], were installed in the South Docks.

The advantages of electric capstans, such as the Stothert & Pitt type 3.10(A10), are economy of power over a wide range of loading and the relatively low cost of generating or purchasing in bulk the motive power. High capital and maintenance costs, arising from the complicated nature of the machinery are, however, drawbacks. Moreover, electrical apparatus is much more vulnerable to the effects of the damp or wet conditions prevalent in maritime installations. The motor of the capstan illustrated is installed in a concrete watertight pit, with the manhole covers sealed and bolted down, and very small inspection covers. The motor is mounted horizontally and connected to the gearbox by a six pin coupling; the capstan head is turned by a worm and spur gear drive connected to a bevel gear.

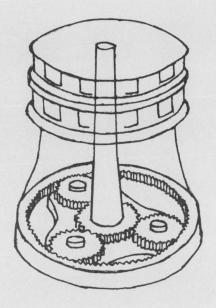

Figure 5

11

It is likely that the first capstans constructed for the dock estate were fashioned by the shipwrights and millwrights directly employed by the Dock Trustees for work on the docks. The development of hydraulic engines for capstans later precluded dockyard manufacture of such sophisticated machinery, and outside orders were placed. The records of the dock estate contain the following references to installations and orders:

1843 Capstans fitted in Kings Basin
1847 Capstans fitted in north entrance of Albert Dock and Salthouse Dock
1860 14 Capstans ordered for various docks
1861 Two double purchase capstans ordered for river gates at Coburg Dock
1863 4 capstans fitted at the south side of the Canning Half Tide Dock
1865 Hydraulic capstans ordered for east side of Wapping Dock south entrance
1881 11 ton hydraulic capstans fitted in Canning Half Tide Dock
1888 7 hydraulic capstans ordered for Toxteth Dock
1900 Hydraulic capstans fitted in new passage between Coburg and Queens Docks
1902 Hydraulic capstans ordered for Brunswick River entrances
1903 Hydraulic capstans fitted in Herculaneum Dock

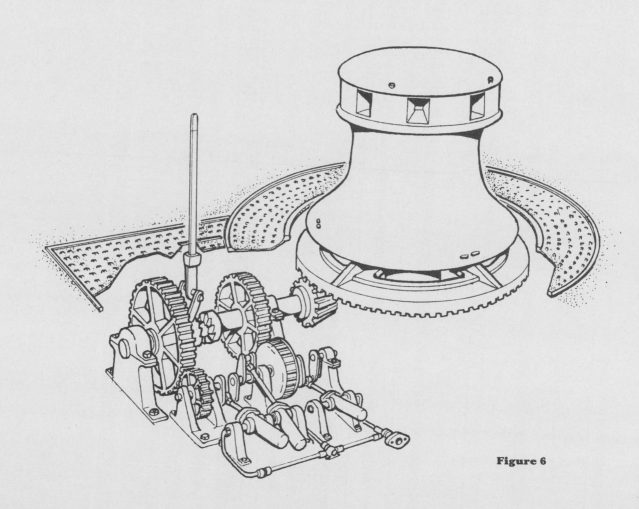

Figure 6

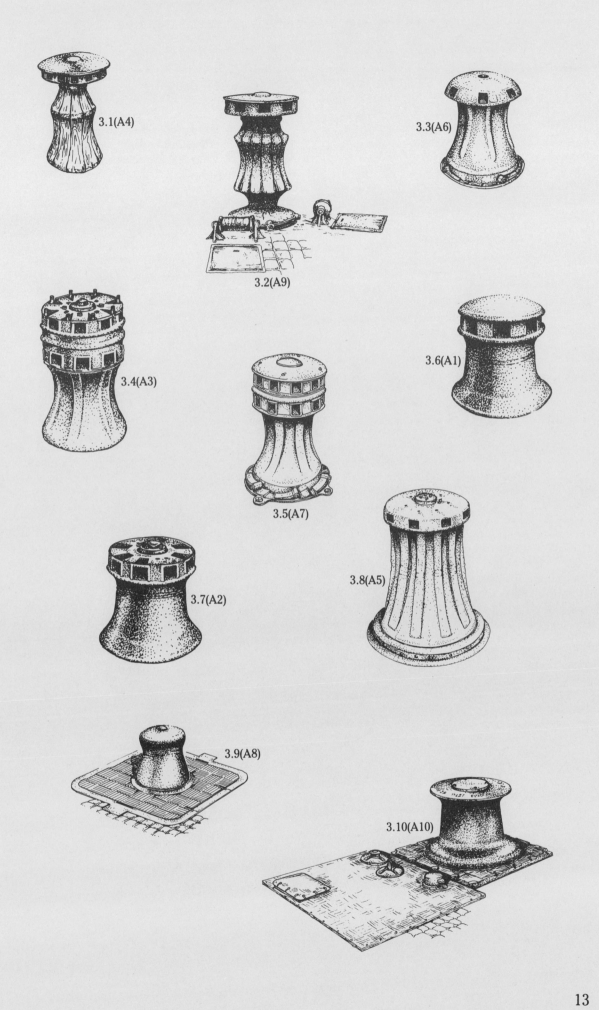

3.1(A4)

3.2(A9)

3.3(A6)

3.4(A3)

3.5(A7)

3.6(A1)

3.7(A2)

3.8(A5)

3.9(A8)

3.10(A10)

13

4.0 Winches

The winch gear first installed in the eighteenth century docks probably consisted of copies of the winding machinery found then on ships, that is, windlasses. The basic design of winches did not alter dramatically over the ensuing centuries, but technological advances in the iron industry and the development of hydraulic power both contributed to more efficient operation of the rudimentary machines. It seems that it was not until 1808 that chains instead of ropes were used as the cables by which dock gates were wound open and closed: 'The Surveyor having reported that the improved iron chain which was ordered as an experiment to be used at the cranes in the stone quarries has been found to answer extremely well. It is ordered that the Surveyor be authorised to procure similar chains for the cranes in the other quarries and also that an experiment be made of the same chains for the dock gates in lieu of the ropes now used'. (*Dock Committee Minutes*, 8 April 1808). It was not until about the same time that wooden drawbridges across dock entrances were superseded by iron swing bridges.

The winding engines illustrated are typical examples of nineteenth century gear used to operate dock gates and swing bridges. By the latter part of the century, the gates and bridges were swung by hydraulic jiggers. The old fashioned engines have not been superseded entirely, however, and winches of the type 4.4(W1) are still in use today in the parts of the North Docks which date from the 1840's and 1850's.

Type 4.1(W3) is a manual windlass used to swing bridges and, in a few instances, to operate clough paddles. The rotation of its horizontal upper axle is transmitted by a pair of bevel gears and a vertical spindle to a quay-level cog which, in turn, acts upon a carved toothed rack fixed to the back of the bridge. The machine illustrated (3ft 8in high) was cast at the Haigh Foundry, Wigan, Lancashire in the 1840's and installed then at the Albert Dock and the rebult passages of the Duke's Dock, Liverpool. Extra purchase can be obtained by fitting a crank handle to the square end of the axle where it protrudes through the casing.

Type 4.2(W2) is a standard manual winch comprising two main axles, the lower one (near quay level) carrying the chain-drum between a large gear wheel and a brake wheel, and the upper one carrying a small cog which meshes with the large gear. The winch is turned by means of removable crank-handles on either side of the machine; a friction shoe acts upon the brake wheel. The winding chain is led from the winding drum to a dock gate through a culvert built in the masonry of the quay wall, and two winches per gate leaf are needed to open and close the leaves. The action of the winches is complementary, with the chain from one being unwound by the opposing winding of the other. The two winches must be situated on opposite sides of the passage. When the dock gates are open, the chains from the slack winches lie on the floor of the passage so that ships can move through the passage without fouling the chains. The side plates of the 3ft 8in high type .2(W2) winch are cast iron; the curved crab cover plates and access doors are wrought iron. The machinery is cast iron. Its gearing

ratio is approximately 8:1, although other types have the choice of two ratios.

Type 4.3(W5) consists of two manual winches (4.2(W2)) placed back to back inside one casing. This type of installation usually appears on the islands built between double (that is, parallel) dock entrances.

Type 4.4(W1) is a type 4.2(W2) mechanism which was converted to hydraulic operation by means of the addition in the 1880's of three in-line oscillating pistons supplied by Sir W G Armstrong & Co. The hydraulic engine is housed in a 4ft 9in x 4ft 10in x 1ft 8in iron box net to the original installation and acts on the gears provided in the manually operated machine. This type of engine has no reversing gears. It if fitted with a dog-toothed clutch, on its main axle, which is engaged by moving the operating lever to the 'pull' position. When the lever is moved to the 'stay' or 'slacken' position, it disengages the clutch and the engine freewheels. In this mode, the chain-drum can be either allowed to run freely by the motion of the opposing winch or locked by the hand brake.

Type 4.5(W4) was developed following the conversion to hydraulic operation of type 4.4(W1). The engine and wheel-work have been placed in a covered well so that only the operating lever obtrudes at quay level. In a shallow, semi-circular depression adjacent to the main well is a capstan head. In the event of engine failure, the cover plate was lifted and four capstan bars were inserted in the head at a predetermined angle of about 30° to the horizontal.

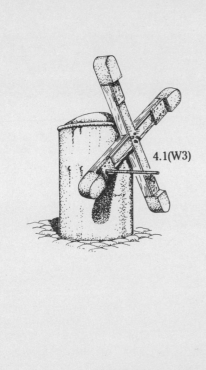

4.1(W3)

4.2(W2)

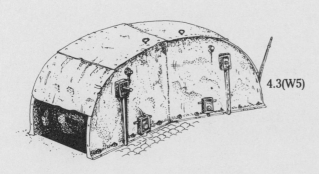

4.3(W5)

4.4(W1)

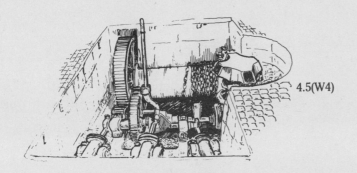

4.5(W4)

5.0 Jiggers

Hydraulic jiggers are amongst the most common machines to be found on the docks, where they activate gates, bridges and cranes. 'Jigger' is the common name given to the hydraulic multiplier which is an hydraulic assembly fitted with sheaves (that is, pulley wheels) at both of its ends. The assembly consists of a ram which travels up and down inside a hollow cylinder as a result of pressure water being admitted to the cylinder and forcing the ram to move. The ram travel can be multiplied by running the operating chain around the pulley wheels situated at the base of the cylinder and the end of the ram respectively. The multiplication factor is directly related to the number of sheaves: if there are two wheels at each end, there will be four lengths of operating chain passing between them and a crane load can be moved through four times the distance that the ram extends. Three sheaves at each end will give a multiplication factor of six, and so on for any number of sheaves, although practical constraints usually limit the maximum to four at each end. However, the multiplication by sheaves results in a related reduction of power: a jigger fitted with three sheaves at each end needs to exert a force in excess of six times the load in order to lift it.

The chain is fixed at one end to a stationary part of the jigger; it is passed around the sheaves before the free end is led to, say, the crane jib. In the case of a crane, the extension of the ram shortens the length of chain available to depend from the end of the jib, and the attached load is raised as the chain is retraced. The jigger can act in only one direction, that is, in the case cited, it can only lift. If the machine is mounted vertically the ram returns to a fully retracted position within the cylinder as a result of the pull of gravity on the ram and on the unladen chain and/or a counterweight fixed to the end of the chain, immediately above the hook. If it is mounted horizontally other means must govern its retraction.

The cylinder, ram and sheaves of a typical jigger are made of cast iron. The slide valve which controls the admission and exhaust of water is brass. Several types of seal have been used to stop water escaping from between the ram and the walls of the cylinder. A machine which depends upon water pressure to work can only be as efficient as the seal which contains the water within it. Joseph Bramah's pioneering experiments in the application of hydraulic power resulted in the development of an hydraulic press (patented in 1795) which owed its success to the fitment of a U-shaped leather ring in a groove at the top of the cylinder. Contrary to the behaviour of other seals, which leaked more as they were subjected to greater pressure, the U-leather became tighter under higher pressures because its walls were forced apart and against the sides of the ram. Later, greased cotton or hemp were fitted into a stuffing box at the end of the cylinder and tightened with a gland, which had the advantage over the annular U-leather of being accessible for tightening from outside the cylinder. Joints between stationary parts were sealed with gaskets made of canvas, india rubber, gutta-percha, copper or lead.

Types 5.1(Y2) and 5.1(Y3) were manufactured in the 1880's by W G Armstrong, Mitchell & Co Ltd of Newcastle-upon-Tyne, although several manufacturers, principally Tannett Walker & Co and John Abbot & Co designed jiggers of a similar type. These are the most common types of hoisting jigger for warehouse cranes. The rods which guide the cross-head of the ram have stops fitted at the ends and these rods are connected by levers to the slide valve controlling the jigger, thereby acting as a fail-safe mechanism to prevent over-extension of the ram. A schematic representation of the relationship between a warehouse jigger and a wall crane is shown in fig 7. The slewing rams at either side of type 5.1(Y2) are small jiggers with a chain passing between them via a wheel on the crane post (see 6.6(E2) in CRANES). The valve which controls them is arranged so that one ram is always admitting water as the other is exhausting, so they are always in complementary positions. Type 5.1(Y2) has only two sheaves at either end giving it a greater power than 5.1(Y3) which has three at each end. This type of jigger was manufactured in various sizes, but an average cylinder length is 5ft 6in. It can be operated from any floor of the building by means of a system of wall-mounted pulleys and chains.

Type 5.2(Y4) is an horizontal crane operating jigger with three cylinders and a long, single-acting ram to return the jigger to its neutral position when exhausting, by pushing against the support of the ram sheaves. Single cylinder jiggers exert the same effort upon the load regardless of its weight, which is evidently very wasteful for light loads, so this jigger has three cylinders to give it

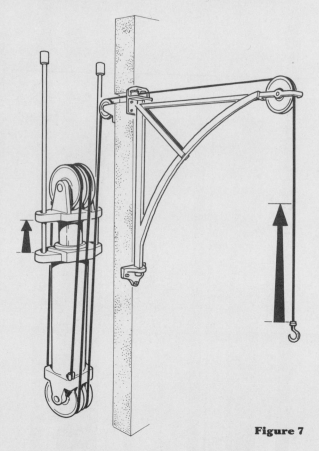

Figure 7

two different power outputs. For light loads, water is admitted to the two outer cylinders only, and for heavier loads, all three cylinders are open to the water inlet.

Type 5.3(Y1) was made in about 1900 by Tannett Walker & Co Ltd of Leeds. It is an horizontal jigger for operating lock gates. In this application one jigger is needed to open each gate leaf and another (on the opposite side of the passage) is needed to close it. As with the crab winches four jiggers are required for the operation of each set of gates. Each machine is sunk into a well about 8ft below the level of the quay and its chain emerges from the wall of the passage about 20ft up from the level of the dock floor. The gate opening jiggers are shorter than those which close the gates and do not have any auxiliary jiggers bolted to their cylinders; both of these differences are readily explained when the operation of the gates is considered (see fig 8). If the gates are closed, both of the closing jiggers (J1 and J2) will be fully extended. When the opening jiggers (J3 and J4) are activated and the closing jiggers are set to exhaust, the former extend until the gates are fully open. The closing jiggers will have retracted by an equal amount, but, as the chains are attached at the horizontal centre-line of the gates (to avoid unnecessary torque at the gate heel posts), the two closing chains (A) would remain stretched across the dock about 20ft above the floor. In order to remove this impediment, the auxiliary jigger (JA) bolted to the gate-closing jiggers has a chain fixed at one end to its own cylinder and at its other end to the cross-head of the main jigger ram. The auxiliary jigger pulls the main ram back to its fully-retracted position, allowing the chain to slacken and fall by its own weight to the bottom of the dock. When the gates are closed, the closing jiggers must extend not only

enough to close the gates, but also enough to first take up the slack in the chains lying on the dock passage floor. They are, consequently, longer than the opening jiggers. Type 5.3(Y1) is a gate closing jigger and has three sheaves at each end. The cross-head of the ram is so large that it needs to run on rails. The auxiliary jigger has two sheaves on its ram and one at the base of its cylinder. The extended length of the whole assembly can vary from 30ft to 50ft depending on the size of the gates which it must move.

Type 5.4(Y5) is a bridge-swinging jigger using steel wire cables instead of chains. These jiggers are always found side by side in pairs (usually in a concrete box adjacent to the well where the pivot of the swing bridge is situated). The wire cable is fixed to the cylinder of one jigger and passes over its sheave and back to the slewing drum, or turntable, of the bridge. This guides the wire back to the second jigger where it passes over the sheave and is secured to the jigger cylinder. When the bridge is open, one jigger is fully extended and the other fully retracted. As the bridge swings, the jiggers are always in complementary positions, one extending, the other exhausting and so a constant torque is exerted on the bridge slewing drum until the jiggers come to the ends of their travel and the bridge is closed.

Types 5.5(Y6) and 5.5(Y7) were made circa 1900 by Francis Morton and Co Ltd of Liverpool. These are simply different sizes of the same jigger and are used to swing bridges. They use wire cable instead of chains and are situated in a pit beneath the well in which the bridge swings.

Type 5.6(Y8) is a bridge-swinging jigger whose fully extended length is approximately 30ft. When it is retracted it is approximately 18ft long, and it, too, uses steel wire cables.

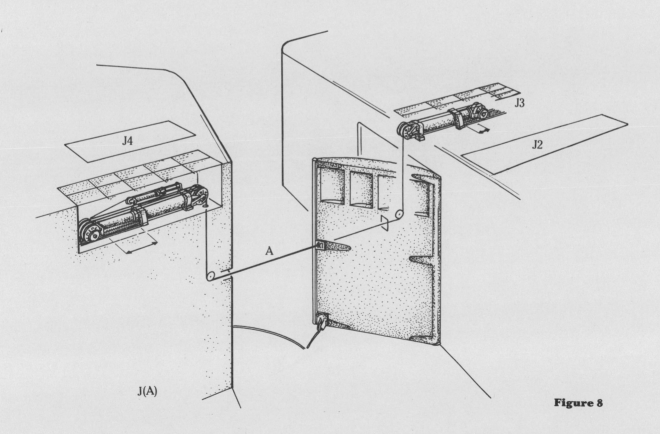

Figure 8

17

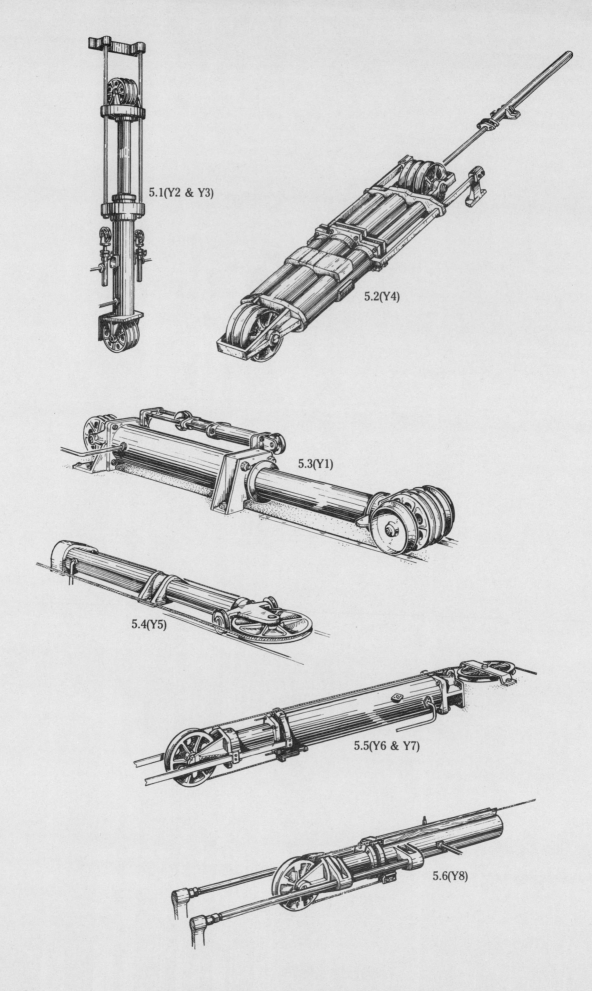

5.1(Y2 & Y3)

5.2(Y4)

5.3(Y1)

5.4(Y5)

5.5(Y6 & Y7)

5.6(Y8)

18

6.0 Cranes

Nineteenth century crane design was based on contemporary understanding of the strength and properties of the structural materials then available. The standard rigid triangle form of crane jib had evolved from the earlier derrick which consisted fo a spar set at an angle to an anchor post, with its head steadied by guys and furnished with suitable tackle and purchases (6.1(E12)). The greater strength of the triangular jib derived from the inflexibility of its geometry and its members.

In calculating the stresses on the principal members of a triangular jib, the designer assumed that a load was suspended from the jib. This assumption had to be made to exclude the tensile forces within the operating chain from the calculation; if the chain was included, it would have to be considered as an extra member of the jib. The weight of the suspended load was represented diagrammatically (see fig 9) by a vertical line graduated with an arbitrary scale. This line was taken as the diagonal ofa parallelogram whose sides were subsequently constructed by drawing lines parallel to the principal members; the lengths of the sides of the parallelogram would then represent (to the same scale as that drawn on the diagonal) the stresses in the corresponding members of the jib. These stresses were clearly tensile in the upper side of the jib and compressive in the lower.

Fg 9 illustrates a worked example of the above method. It is based on a wooden crane (fig 10) from the dock yard forge at Coburg Dock, Liverpool. In this case, there is no operating chain so the load does, in fact, depend directly from the iron traveller at the end of the jib. For the purposes of the following calculation, the traveller is assumed to rest at the junction of the upper jib member and the strut. The line AC has been divided into ½ in sections, each of which represents 10 cwt. The line AB has been drawn along the strut and the line BC has been drawn parallel to the upper jib member so as to intersect AC at C. In the triangle thus formed, the length of the line

(AB) parallel to the strut gives the force in the strut, and the length of the line (BC) parallel to the upper member gives the force in that member on the same scale as that marked on line AC. AB is 2.3in—long and BC is 1.75in—long.

The force in the strut will be:
$$\frac{2.3''}{0.5''} \times 10 \text{ cwt} = 46 \text{ cwt}$$

The force in the upper member will be:
$$\frac{1.75''}{0.5''} \times 10 \text{ cwt} = 35 \text{ cwt}$$

A diagram of the forces could also have been drawn from A to D and then from D to C to yield the same answers.

The diagonal AC is the resultant of the two forces represented by AB and BC (or AD and DC). To reach point C, forces must follow either path ABC or path ADC as indicated by the arrows. The forces corresponding to the upper member of the jib tend to pull it away from the crane post, thereby putting the member in tension. The forces corresponding to the strut push it towards the crane post, subjecting this member to compression.

By the mid-nineteenth century, most cranes were made of iron. Then it was known that the compressive strengths of cast and wrought iron were 48 tons per sq in and 11 tons per sq in respectively. It was also known that the tensile limit of cast iron was 7.2 tons per sq in and that wrought iron became permanently deformed in tension under loads in excess of 10 tons per sq in. Thus cast iron was the material chosen for jib members in compression and wrought iron was used for those in tension.

It was only after numerous failures and mill collapses that other precepts governing the use of structural ironwork were defined: wrought iron ties should never be subjected to stresses in excess of 3 tons per sq in or 2 tons per sq in if brakes were used for lowering the load; cast

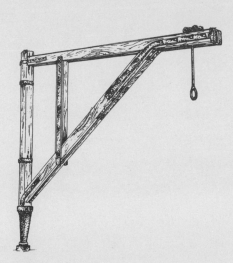

Figure 9

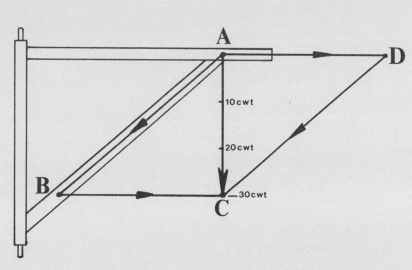

Figure 10

iron cranes should not handle loads greater than 10% of their breaking weight or 5% if brakes were applied. These precepts were used to determine the Safe Working Load (SWL) of each type of crane.

Natural fibre crane operating ropes were replaced by chains made of best wrought iron in circular section. Repeated passage over pulleys and winding drums caused the links to become brittle and susceptible to fracture, a phenomenon known as work-hardening. In order to prevent chain failure caused by work-hardening, operating chains were annealed (heated to red heat and allowed to cool slowly) every six months, to restore their tensile strength.

The care taken by the crane designer and the chain tester were often rendered pointless by the failure of crane hooks. These were often designed by the smiths who forged them and they were often the wrong shape, or too small. It was asserted in 1850 that more men were killed and more cargoes lost as a result of broken cane hooks than as a result of any other single machine failure.

Formally derived from a ship's davit type 6.2 (E7) is a small jib without a chain or rope, used to drag suspended crane loads onto the quayside. It is fixed to the pillar of the warehouse arcade (see fig 11) by two wrought iron hoops fitted with sockets in which it pivots freely. Thus it can be swung out by hand to retrieve loads suspended from cranes above it and haul them into the arched warehouse bay.

Type 6.3 (E3) is a single iron casting, dating from 1846, of the type known variously as a cantilever crane or vault crane. In a cantilever, the maximum stress in the jib is at the junction with the crane post so the jib is at its deepest (ie the whole height of the crane post) in this position. As the stress decreases towards the free end, so the depth of the jib diminishes. The circular lattice work affords maximum strength with minimum weight. Originally a hand crane, it was converted to hydraulic operation in 1882. It is bolted to the wall and operated by the type 5.1 (Y3) jigger which has three sheaves at either end giving the assembly of jigger and crane a SWL of 20 cwt. The slewing mechanism was not converted from manual to hydraulic operation. Such cranes are usually found at the ground or first floor levels of warehouses.

Type 6.4 (E6) is the simplest form of crane jib. The strut is bolted to the crane post at its base and the tie bars at the top are pinned at either end, with a single bolt separating them at their centres. This hand operated crane serves only the lower floors of warehouses.

Type 6.5 (E4) is a mid-nineteenth century hand operated wall crane found high upon warehouse walls. It performs the function of swinging loads into various levels of warehouses and this slewing is achieved by means of a pair of bevel gears at the centre of the crane post, the gears being turned by a crank-handle fitted over a boss protruding into the warehouse from the back-plate of the crane.

Type 6.6 (E2) is a wall crane found mainly at first or second floor levels of warehouses. It is hydraulically operated by means of a type 5.1 (Y2) jigger. Its function is to lift loads from ground level into the lower floors of the warehouse by swinging over across the open doorways. The strut and crane post are cast in one piece and the tension member is a bar of wrought iron sandwiched by, and bolted to, two wrought iron strips. Slewing, or turning, of the crane is by the action of a chain passing over the wheel fixed to the top of the crane post (see 5.1 (5.2) jigger for slewing). Because a high lift is not required to the first two floors, this jigger needs only two sheaves at either end. This increases the power of the jigger over one with three sheaves at each end and so this crane has a SWL of 30 cwt.

Type 6.7 (E10) is an hydraulic wall crane operated by the type 5.1 (Y3) jigger and slewed by hand. Its compression strut and tie bars are of bolted cast and wrought iron respectively, rivetted to the crane post via cast iron corner plates. Situated near the lower floors of warehouses, its SWL is 20 cwt. The structure, if not the appearance, of type 6.8 (E11) is similar to that of type 6.7 (E10). It is powered by the type 5.1 (Y3) hydraulic jigger and its SWL is 20 cwt.

Type 6.9 (E1) is a large hydraulically powered quayside crane which operates within an arched warehouse bay (see fig 11) and is fixed to one of the supporting columns of the arch by a wrought iron hoop. The top of the cast iron crane post fits into a socket on the column hoop; the base of the crane post pivots below the level of the quay.

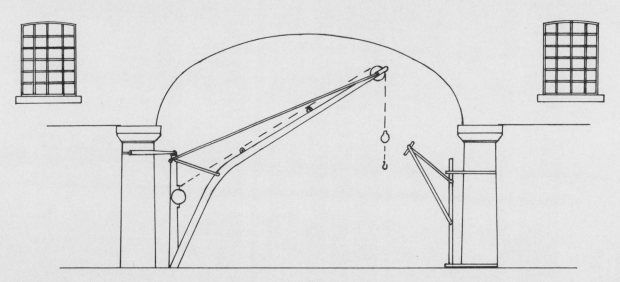

Figure 11

20

The dog-legged jib-piece is formed from two side plates of cast iron separated by, and rivetted to, a wrought iron spacer plate, and the upper members, or tension rods, of the jib are of circular section wrought iron. The chain passes up through the centre of the hollow crane post from the operating jigger 5.2 (Y4). The crane has a SWL of 2 tons.

Type 6.10 (E5) is a more sophisticated assembly which contains its own hoisting jigger between the two bolted cast iron plates of its crane post, and a dog-legged compression strut, similar in construction to that of type 6.9 (E1). Slewing is made possible by pulling the chain which passes around the wheel fixed to the base of the crane post, and may be done manually or, more usually, by means of hydraulic rams.

Hydraulic slewing is effected by means of two parallel rams installed horizontally in a shallow box on the floor inside the warehouse; these rams are some 4ft long when retracted and some 5½ft long when extended. Type 6.10 (E5) has a SWL of 30 cwt.

Type 6.11 (E8) is an electrically operated quayside crane with a hollow cast iron cantilever jib projecting from the top of its crane post. Although it occupies a fixed position on the quayside, it has a long rake (radius) relative to its height and it can be turned through 360° by means of the electric motor. It uses steel wire cable rather than a chain.

Type 6.12 (E9) is a moveable electric quayside crane with a motor by Joseph Booth & Bros Ltd of Leeds. The power is transmitted to the lifting and slewing mechanisms by means of bevel gears. The jib is rigidly cast in iron and held by two circular section wrought iron tie rods. The crane can be wheeled to any position within the warehouse arch and made secure by lowering the corner jacks. Fitted with steel cable, its SWL is 12 cwt when using one wire and 24 cwt if using two.

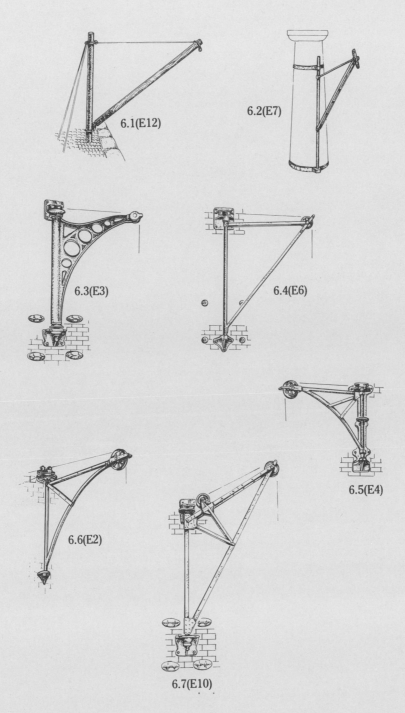

6.1(E12)

6.2(E7)

6.3(E3)

6.4(E6)

6.5(E4)

6.6(E2)

6.7(E10)

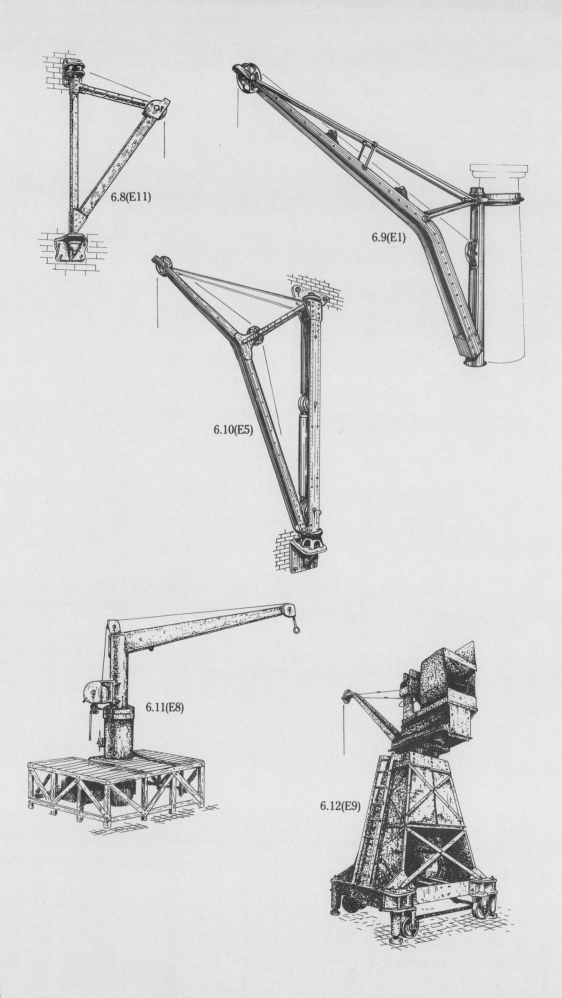

6.8(E11)

6.9(E1)

6.10(E5)

6.11(E8)

6.12(E9)

22

7.0 Fairleads

Fairleads, or snatch heads (also sometimes known as idler wheels in the Liverpool Docks) are used to alter the direction of a rope or cable being led between a vessel in a dock and a capstan or bollard on the quay. They were usually manufactured by firms who supplied the capstans. When these mechanisms were first installed to facilitate warping ships at pier heads, they were called 'revolving mushrooms' — a description which needs no amplification to give a precise idea of their function and form. It is thought that the term 'idler wheel' arose from the early use of the fairleads as tiny mooring posts by barges and flats 'idling' at dock entrances whilst awaiting their turns to proceed into or out of the docks.

Type 7.1 (R1) consists of a 17in diameter head above a wheel which rotates on a spindle, and a four pronged baseplate pinned to the quay with bolts approximately 18in long. It is made of cast iron and stands 8⅔in above the quay surface. An improved version of this type features roller bearings as well as the standard feature of a removable head which gives interior access for the purpose of changing the grease packing.

The top of the type 7.2 (R2) assembly is of the same pattern and specification as type 7.1 (R1), but its baseplate incorporates a platform which gives the idler wheel as overall height of 13in.

The head and rotating wheel, which are separate in types 7.1(R1) and 7.2(R2), are cast in a single piece in type 7.3(R3). This single iron casting rotates on a spindle. The assembly is 15in in diameter and 10in high with the longer barrel allowing a rope to be passed around the wheel more than once and thereby affording greater control.

Type 7.4(R4) is made of cast steel. Its head diameter is 10in, overall height is 7in and the base plate is 18in square. This pattern also allows more than one turn of rope to be passed round it and the rounded flange at its base prevents any scuffing of the rope on the base plate or the bolts which secure it.

Type 7.5(R5) is 10in high, cast iron, with a diameter of 8in. It can accommodate more than one turn of rope and is cast with a flange to prevent scuffing of ropes on the quay. The whole unit turns upon a central spindle to which it is fixed by a taper or split-pin.

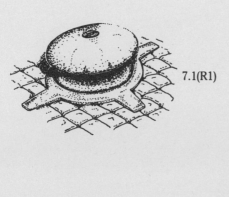

7.1(R1)

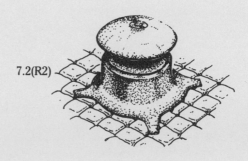

7.2(R2)

7.3(R3)

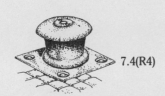

7.4(R4)

7.5(R5)

8.0 Chain Posts

The 1796 *Liverpool Guide* explained that guard chains along the edge of the docks . . . became necessary to prevent strangers and others falling in in the night, from missing their way, from intoxication, etc . . . In 1807 The West India Association was given permission to fix up temporary iron stanchions and chains so as to enclose a part of the dock quays for the purposes of landing, weighing, taring and sampling coffee and cocoa. In later years, safety legislation ensured the provision of barriers on quay edges.

Nineteenth century fencing consisted typically of cast or wrought iron or mild steel standards with round or square eyes for chains and a square section base which was embedded in the quay. Some standards were set temporarily in cast iron sockets, and others were installed permanently. Some of the permanent standards, such as type 8.1(P1), were often cast with as great an extent below ground as above. The total length of this type of stanchion is some 6ft, the buried portion, 3ft long, tapers

from an 8in square section at ground level to a 12in square section at the bottom.

Holes in posts of sufficient diameter to permit the threading of chain necessarily permit also the running of chain, so that pressure applied to a point on the chain will cause it to sag. This failure can be avoided by fitting accessories including the chain collars, wedges and single and double chain hooks illustrated.

Table 3

Type	Material	Type	Material
8.1(P1)	Cast Iron	8.7(P7)	Wrought iron
8.1(P2)	Cast iron	8.8(P8)	Steel
8.3(P3)	Wrought iron	8.9(P9)	Steel
8.4(P4)	Wrought iron	8.10(P10)	Cast iron
8.5(P5)	Granite	8.11(P11)	Cast iron
8.6(P6)	Cast iron		

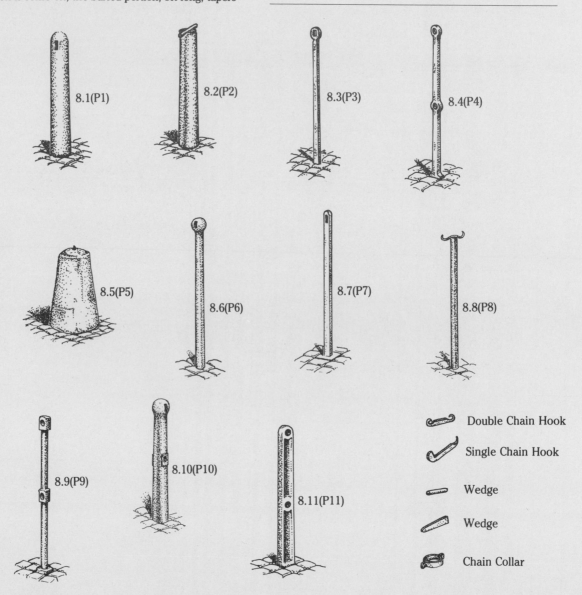

24

9.0 Lights

In 1820 The Liverpool Gas Light Company sought permission to lay branch gas pipes along the quays of the Old Dock, the east quay of Georges Dock and the quays of Georges Dock Passage and the Dry (later Canning) Dock. The members of the Dock Committee were opposed to the plan because of damage the excavations would do to the pavements. But a year later Mr Taylor, one of the patentees of oil gas, was invited to undertake a survey and prepare an estimate of the cost of introducing this type of gas on the dock estate, and shortly the Liverpool quays were illuminated by gas. In 1838 the Dock Surveyor reported '. . . that each of the gas companies had become liable to the following fines under their contracts for lighting the dock quays, viz, The Liverpool New Gas and Coke Company for the number of lamps that have not been lighted, or if so, having gone out again, during the quarter ending the 31st March last, being 842, the fines on which at 2/6d each amount to £105.5s.0d and The Liverpool Gas Light Company for 36 lamps . . . amounting to £4.10s.0d'. By 1844 the contract price for lamplighting was £4.17s.6d per lamp per annum. The vaults of the new Albert Dock Warehouses were lit by gas in 1846.

In the early 1890's The Liverpool Electric Supply Company Limited began to provide electricity generating machinery for the South Docks. Their installation at the Albert Dock consisted of an engine, boiler and dynamo placed in the former hydraulic engine house, and cables laid throughout the warehouses, '. . . with sockets placed at convenient positions in each room for the attachment of flexible leads to supply portable 50 candle power lamps.' (*Dock Engineer's Reports*, 1895). Sockets for leads to be used on board vessels in the dock were also provided. From 1914 the individual generating plants were dispensed with and new electric cables were laid on the dock estate to receive Corporation current.

Type 9.1(L1) is a cast iron gas-lamp standard. The hollow post conceals and protects the gas feed pipe to the lamp. The regulator and burner are attached to the end of the angled bracket which acts as an extension of the feed pipe. A groove and projecting bar on the post provided the lamplighter with a safe point against which to lean his ladder.

Accessories (a), (b), and (c) are variations of the basic burner holder. Since lamp standards were usually provided at pier heads where capstans were installed for hauling vessels through dock passages, a cast iron lattice frame (d) was fitted to posts in these positions for vertical storage of capstan bars. The height of the lamp standard can be increased by fitting an hexagonal cast iron plinth (e).

Type 9.2(L2), 9.3(L3) and 9.4(L4) are all iron standards for electric lights. The box at the base of type 9.4(L4) contains the switching mechanism which chould have been operated manually by a lamp lighter or automatically by clockwork and a timing device.

Type 9.5(L5) is a wrought iron bracket, fixed to the outside walls of warehouses, to hold a gas lamp burner. This pattern dates from the 1840's.

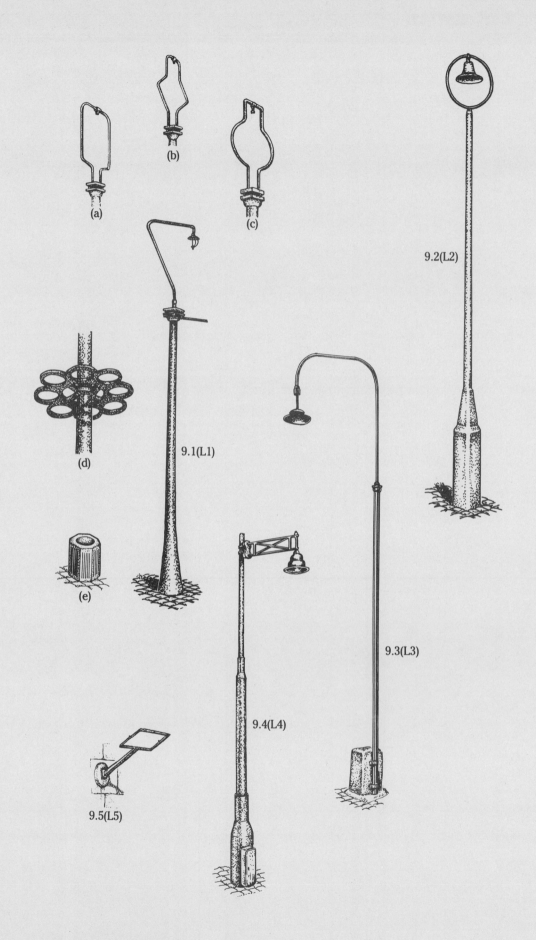

(a)

(b)

(c)

(d)

(e)

9.1(L1)

9.2(L2)

9.3(L3)

9.4(L4)

9.5(L5)

26

10.0   Cloughs

Sluices for the management of water levels were incorporated in the gates and pier heads of the docks in Liverpool from the eighteenth century. These sluices served a number of purposes: to equalise water pressure on either side of the dock gates; to lower the level of water within the dock to match the river level and thus enable the opening of the gates; to facilitate the movement of gates; to alter the water levels between gates at locked entrances; to drain dry docks. Additionally, extensive sluice systems were built in the early twentieth century at the new river entrances to the south Docks in an effort to utilise the scouring action of the water passing through the sluices to reduce the accumulations of the Pluckington sandbank. The designer of these systems, the Dock Engineer George Fosbery Lyster, described their operation in 1896: 'The dock sills are laid at the level of 12 feet below datum throughout, and their main entrances and wing walls at Herculaneum are provided with an elaborate system of sluices, carried under a jetty on the riverside . . . alongside the river wall instead of projecting into the River. This has been the means of fully maintaining the sills and fairway open and free from silt . . .' (G F Lyster's Paper to the Liverpool Meeting of the British Association of Science).

Sluice gates or paddles were traditionally made of greenheart, a very hard timber from the West Indies. Their construction was as strong as possible because of the rigorous conditions which they needed to withstand. All joints were made with red lead, and the ends of the timbers caulked wherever a crack, or shake, occurred before being painted with black varnish. Bolt heads and nuts were recessed into the timber, and when screwed up, the recesses were filled with red lead and plugged with greenheart dowels. Two large galvanised eyebolts, for the attachment of lifting spears, were set in the top of the clough before the whole was planed prior to painting. The dimensions of clough paddles vary considerably, but an average, usual size can be taken to be 8ft high by 5ft wide, with a thickness of about 8in at the bottom of the paddle.

Type 10.3(S3) shows an Armstrong hydraulic engine (see under Capstans) connected to a manual pattern clough paddle by means of a geared capstan head running from a bevel-geared driveshaft and incorporating a dog clutch along the shaft to engage and disengage the feed. Should the clough become lodged between its granite jambs or the engine seize, the clough could be disengaged using the dog clutch and then worked manually using capstan bars inserted in the sockets in the capstan head.

The word 'clough' is defined in the *Shorter Oxford English Dictionary* as the erroneous spelling of 'clow', a sluice or dam. From about 1820, however, the paddles have been referred to in both the Liverpool Dock Committee Minutes and contemporary engineering treatises as 'cloughs', so that spelling has been retained in this publication.

A manual clough (10.1(S2)) is activated by means of a hand operated leadscrew on the quayside. The crosshead moves up and down on the action of the leadscrew; the paddles are held in the vertical plane by cast iron 'gib' strips. Manual cloughs are very simple to maintain but very tedious to operate.

An hydraulic clough (10.2(S1)) is operated by an hydraulic piston acting vertically on the cast iron crosshead from which depend the two spears or connecting rods to the paddle. When the sluices are open their crossheads and piston rod heads emerge through cast iron flap doors and stand proud of the quay surface; this aspect of their operation makes it possible to judge from a distance the positions of the sluice gates. Hydraulic cloughs work quickly and easily, but they contain a number of parts, such as seals, which perish readily under harsh conditions. Sometimes a manually operated paddle was installed, in a double sluice, next to an hydraulically operated paddle. When the hand paddle was lowered, the culvert could be dried to give access to the hydraulic paddle so as to effect *in situ* repairs.

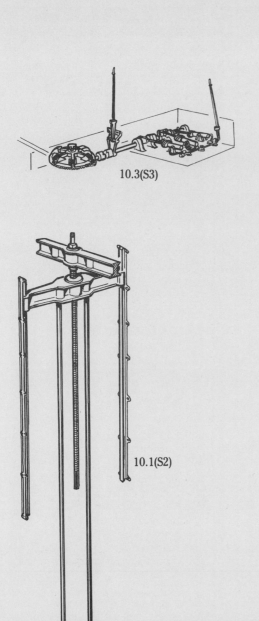

10.3(S3)

10.1(S2)

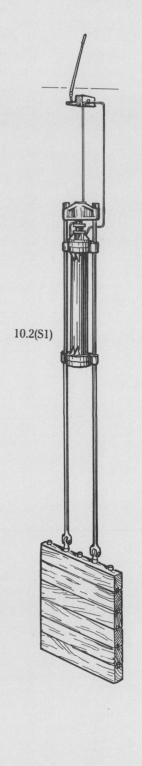

10.2(S1)

11.0 Miscellaneous Fixtures

11.1 *Manhole Covers*

The covers illustrated are typical of the three basic types of cover plate found on the dock estate. Types 11.1, 11.3 and 11.5 are all general purpose covers for hydrant pits, gas valves and hydraulic pipe inspection points. Types 11.2 and 11.4 are used to cover the shafts containing manual clough machinery; the central hole has a removable plug to allow access to the clough lead-screw head. The smaller holes near the corners of the plate allow the clough position indicators to pass through, thus alerting the operator as to the exact position of the paddle within the culvert. Manual cloughs can be operated without removing the manhole covers. Types 11.6 and 11.7 are circular grilles covering the air shafts which are sunk at intervals along some quay walls to allow the sluicing culverts to breathe.

All of these plates are made of cast iron.

11.2 *Cleats*

A cleat is any protrusion, wood or metal, for the sole purpose of securing or making fast a rope or chain. The three illustrated are all quayside cleats but ring cleats were also attached to the drum-heads of primitive capstans (e.g. provision was made for fixing four such cleats to the head of capstan type 3.1). Type 11.8 is a cast iron cleat usually found set into concrete quays at regular intervals between the mooring posts. Type 11.9, is a wrought iron ring cleat found on the copings of older dock walls. These were used as mooring rings for light craft where the absence of any bollards precluded more usual methods of tying up. Type 11.10 is a chain holder.

11.3 *Fuse Box*

Cast iron fuse boxes were installed in the 1890's to serve the new electric lights on the dock estate. They also made convenient points for switching on the lamps before the automatic clockwork timer was introduced for individual lamp standards.

Manhole Covers

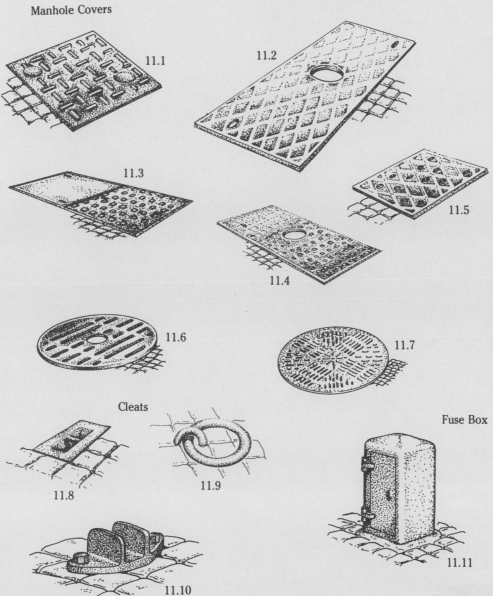

11.1

11.2

11.3

11.5

11.4

11.6

11.7

Cleats

11.8

11.9

11.10

Fuse Box

11.11

12.0 Manufacturers and Suppliers

A definitive work describing the choice, supply, ordering, receipt and use or installation of the materials and machinery for the docks over nearly three centuries would provide an invaluable quarry from which to obtain economic, technological and cybernetic history. The Mersey Docks and Harbour Board Collection, used in conjunction with other archives such as, say, the Boulton and Watt Collection in Birmingham could yield much of the information necessary to compile such a work. This is far from the purpose of the present publication which has been produced as an industrial archaeological sampler and a vehicle for Nick Phillips' illustrations of dockland artefacts. Nevertheless, even a most superficial introduction to the subject of manufacturers and supplies to the dock estate can provide illumination and, of course, interest.

The port of Liverpool was the site of a considerable number of shipbuilding enterprises during the eighteenth and nineteenth centuries. The skills and materials needed to make capstans, bollards and gate machinery were readily available. By at least 1800 the Liverpool Dock Trustees were operating a yard to the west of Salthouse Dock for the dock works. In the early days this yard was removed to Coburg Dock in the late 1830's, the operation became fairly sophisticated. It is important to understand that the dockyard, as it was known locally, was not the Naval shipbuilding yard which the term more generally implies. Liverpool's dockyards had only a few functions in common with the shipbuilding dockyards: shipwrights' shop, smithies, foundries and sawpits/mills. The Liverpool example lacked the mast houses and ponds, and the sail and mould lofts required in a shipyard, but it was provided additionally with the mortar mill and lime kiln needed for dock construction. It is evident from the records that considerable quantities of raw materials were purchased by the Dock Engineer for the fabrication of fixtures or parts of fixtures on the dock estate. The ironwork supplied from the dock yard included gate straps and fittings, chain posts and rudimentary

machinery. Very large castings, or multiple orders, and complex machinery were supplied for the dock works by contractors.

The means of identifying contractors and subsequently placing orders varied considerably. When the Dock Committee began to consider the replacement of wooden draw bridges by iron swing bridges around 1808 the Dock Surveyor was instructed to obtain '. . . proper plans, models and estimates . . .' (*Dock Committee Minutes*, 8th April 1808). The Surveyor produced a drawing of an iron bridge which had been installed at Hull together with a letter from the Secretary of the Hull Docks Company offering to lend a model of their bridge if required.

A contract was eventually let to Messrs Aydon & Elwell of Bradford, Yorkshire, the firm which had supplied the iron bridge at Hull and which, incidentally, had supplied some of the railways for the excavation of the London Docks, Phase I around 1803. Later, when John Rennie was working as consultant engineer to the Dock Trustees, one of his responsibilities was to recommend companies which he deemed competent to tender for iron work contracts. Once Jesse Hartley had been appointed Dock Surveyor, he undertook his own investigations, and it was following his trip to Newcastle-upon-Tyne to see the prototypal quayside crane that he decided to instal hydraulic machinery in his new warehouses at Albert Dock, Liverpool. Nearly forty years later, in 1882, Sir W G Armstrong was still the only one approached by the Sub-committee on dock works to submit a tender for the supply of hydraulic machinery for the new South works (Toxteth, Harrington and Herculaneum Docks). Following the discovery of irregularities in the supply of certain materials to the dock estate in the early 1820's new procedures for advertising for tenders were defined; but these regulations were not applied in later years to the provision of hydraulic machinery, and it was not until the end of the nineteenth century that all contracts were thrown open to competitive tenders.

Representative list of firms supplying dock machinery, ironwork and raw materials for ironwork to the Liverpool docks in the nineteenth century

Name of firm	Item or items supplied	Approximte date/s
J Abbot & Co, Park Works, Gateshead	Capstans	1900
W G Armstrong & Co, Elswick Works Newcastle-upon-Tyne	Hydraulic hoists, cranes, accumulators, jiggers, capstans	1850-1900
Aydon & Elwell, Bradford	Iron bridges	1810
William Bingley & Sons	Iron chains	1810
Blackellar & Mawdsley	Galvanised iron and steel	1850
Brown, Logan & Co	Iron chains	1820
Bury, Curtis & Kennedy	Castings	1840-1850
Butterly Ironworks, Alfreton, Derby	Iron cranes	1810
Carron Co, Glasgow	Castings	1840-1860
Cato, Miller & Co	Ironwork	1850
Chillington Coal & Iron Co, Wolverhampton	Iron rails and bar iron	1840
Coalbrookdale Co, Shropshire	Iron	1850
Cowgill, Comer & Jones	Iron and brass castings	1840-1850
Dalmellington Iron Co, Dalomellington, Western Scotland	Pig iron	1860
Davenport, Grindrod & Patrick	Cranes and castings	1840
Thomas Dove & Co	Ironwork	1820
William Fawcett, Liverpool	Cast iron	1810
Geo. Forrester & Co	Castings	1840
Glenfield & Kennedy, Kilmarnock	Capstans and turnover capstans	1890
Gospel Oak Iron Works, Tipton, Staffordshsire	Mooring and guard posts	1840
Guest & Co, Dowlais Works, Glamorgan	Bar iron	1840
Haigh Foundry Co, Wigan	Castings, iron bridges	1840-1850
John A Haswell	Castings	1840-1850
William Hazeldine, Staffordshire	Iron bridges	1820
Hird, Dawson & Hardy, Low Moor Foundry, Bradford	Iron	1840
James Hodgson & Co	Cranes	1840
Humble & Milcrest, Liverpool	Windlasses	1840
Kempson, Pope & Co	Cast iron chain posts	1820
Kirkstall Forge, Kirkstall, Leeds	Iron bridges	1860
Lee, Bell & Co	Large moveable crane	1840
Mather Dixon & Co	Castings	1830-1840
Mersey Steel & Iron Co, Liverpool	Iron and steel	1840
Francis Morton & Co, Garston	Jiggers, bridges	1890
James Morton & Co	Cast iron work for various purposes	1820-1840
C & A Musker, Liverpool	Capstans, jiggers	1890
Ogden & Barnes, Liverpool	Capstans	1860
Pritt, Case & Butler	Ironwork	1820
W H Sparrow & Co, Bilston Hill, Staffordshire	Iron	1850
Stothert & Pitt, Bath	Electric cranes and capstans	1920
Edward Strong & Co	Ironwork	1820
Tannett Walker & Co Ltd, Leeds	Capstans, jiggers	1890-1900
James Taylor & Co, Birkenhead	Ironwork and cranes	1860-1880
Taylor & Pritt	Ironwork	1810
Toll End Furnace Co, Tipton, Staffordshire	Cast iron chain posts	1820
Whitehaven Haematite Iron Co, Cleator Works, Cumberland	Iron	1850
Thomas Jones Wilkinson	Ironwork	1810
Henry Wood & Co	Chains	1840

Select Bibliography

Blaine, R G, *Hydraulic Machinery,* 1905, Finsbury Technical Manuals

Cornick, H F, *Dock and Harbour Engineering,* 1962, Charles Griffin & Co Ltd, London

Du-Plat-Taylor, F M G, *Docks Wharves and Piers,* 1928, Earnest Benn Ltd, London

Glynn, J, *An Elementary Treatise on the Constructon of Cranes and Machinery, c. 1850,* Published 1854, Reprinted in the *19th Century Engineering* Series, Bath, 1970.